TERRORMAZIA

Yºu are about to arrive at the evil island of Terrormazia. There's treasure here in Crocodile Creek and your task is to reach it before Captain Sharkskin and his pirate gang. But beware! They'll stop you if they can. Terrormazia is a dangerous place so choose your route with care!

HOW TO REACH THE TREASURE

1. You will need a pointer such as a stick for this game. Using your pointer, go through the Magic Tunnel opposite, to the yellow Landing Spot. Now turn the page.

LANDING SPOT

2. Read the maze rules for the Clouds of Chaos.

3. Start at the yellow Landing Spot and make your way through the maze to a Magic Tunnel. If you fail to reach one, go back to the yellow Landing Spot and start again.

4. When you reach a Magic Tunnel, go through it to the Landing Spot and turn to that page. Memorize the colour of the Landing Spot (in case you have to go back to it), read the new maze rules and set off again.

5. You MAY go across Landing Spots but you MAY NOT go across Magic Tunnels.

6. Sometimes you will have to travel backwards. Sometimes you will return to mazes you have visited before. If you find yourself on a particular Landing Spot more than once, aim for a different Magic Tunnel.

If you are lucky or clever you'll land on the treasure. But next time – get there FASTER!

TERRORMAZIA

ANNA NILSEN
illustrated by DOM MANSELL

MAGIC TUNNEL
START HERE

First published 1995 by Walker Books Ltd
87 Vauxhall Walk, London SE1 5HJ

This edition published 2005

2 4 6 8 10 9 7 5 3

Text © 1995 Anna Nilsen. Illustrations © 1995 Dom Mansell

This book has been typeset in Caslon Antique

Printed in China

British Library Cataloguing in Publication Data is available

ISBN-13: 978-1-84428-551-8
ISBN-10: 1-84428-551-0

www.walkerbooks.co.uk

WALKER BOOKS
AND SUBSIDIARIES
LONDON · BOSTON · SYDNEY · AUCKLAND

For William
A.N.

For Rosie
D.M.

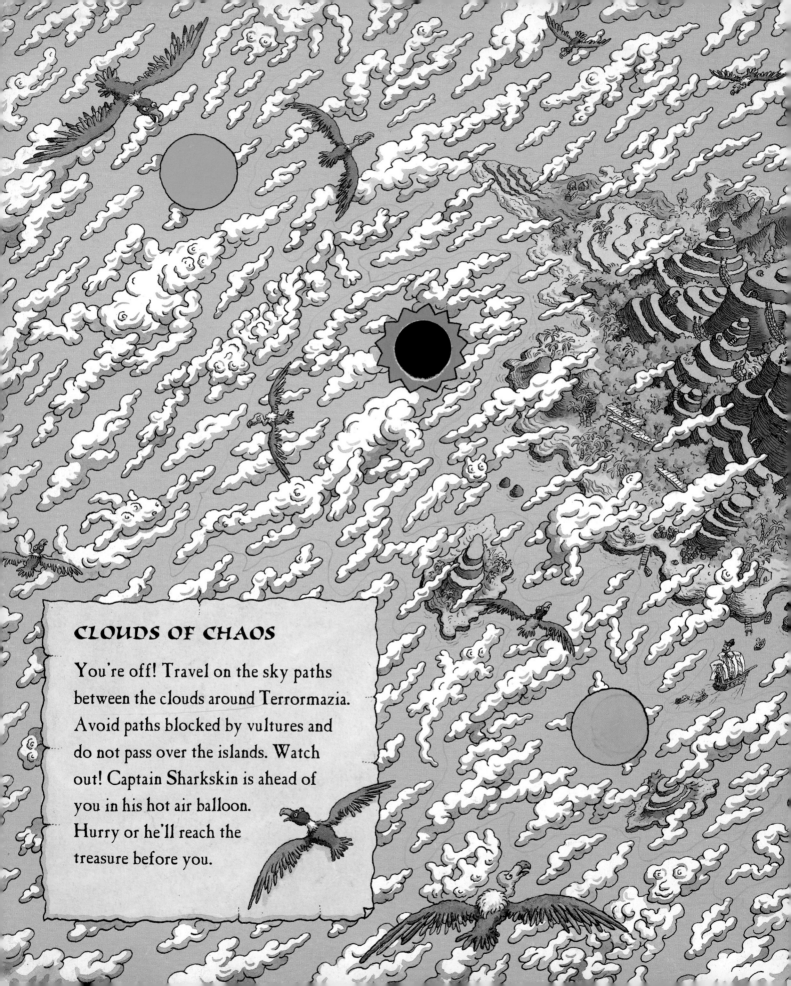

CLOUDS OF CHAOS

You're off! Travel on the sky paths
between the clouds around Terrormazia.
Avoid paths blocked by vultures and
do not pass over the islands. Watch
out! Captain Sharkskin is ahead of
you in his hot air balloon.
Hurry or he'll reach the
treasure before you.

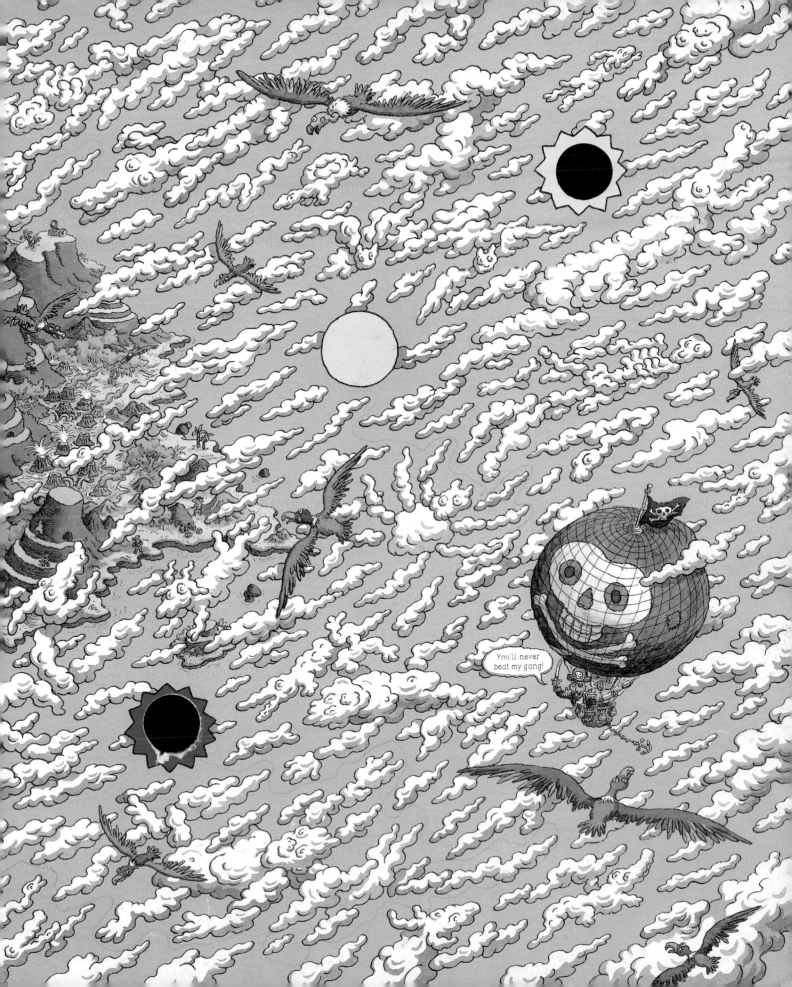

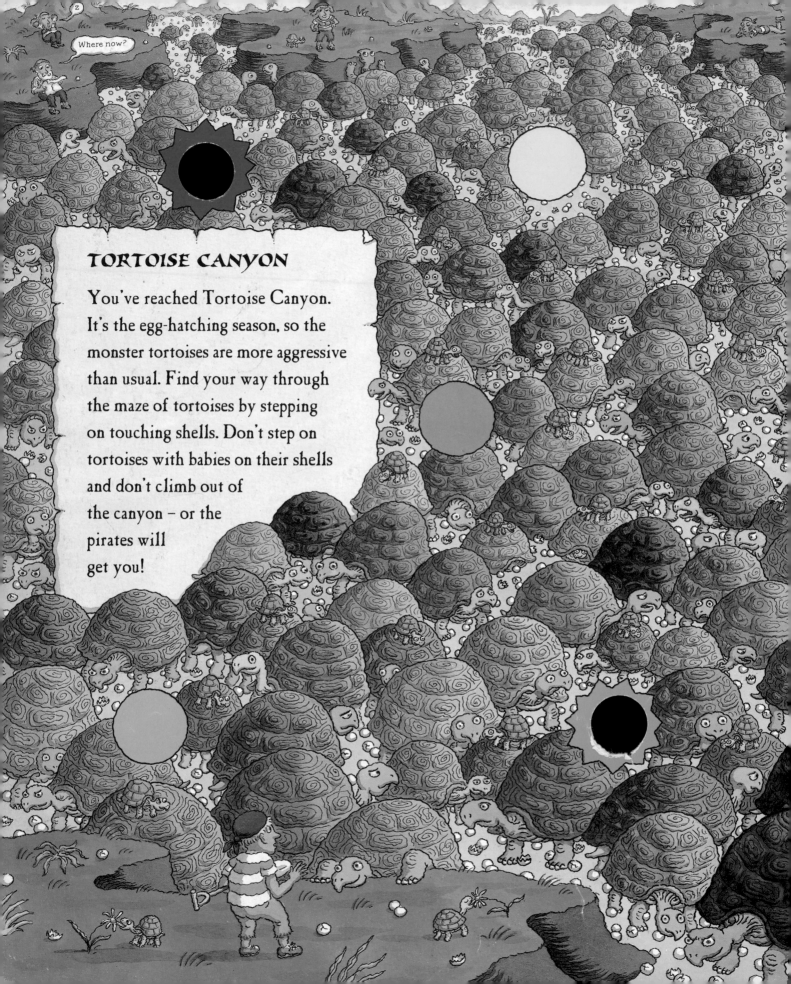

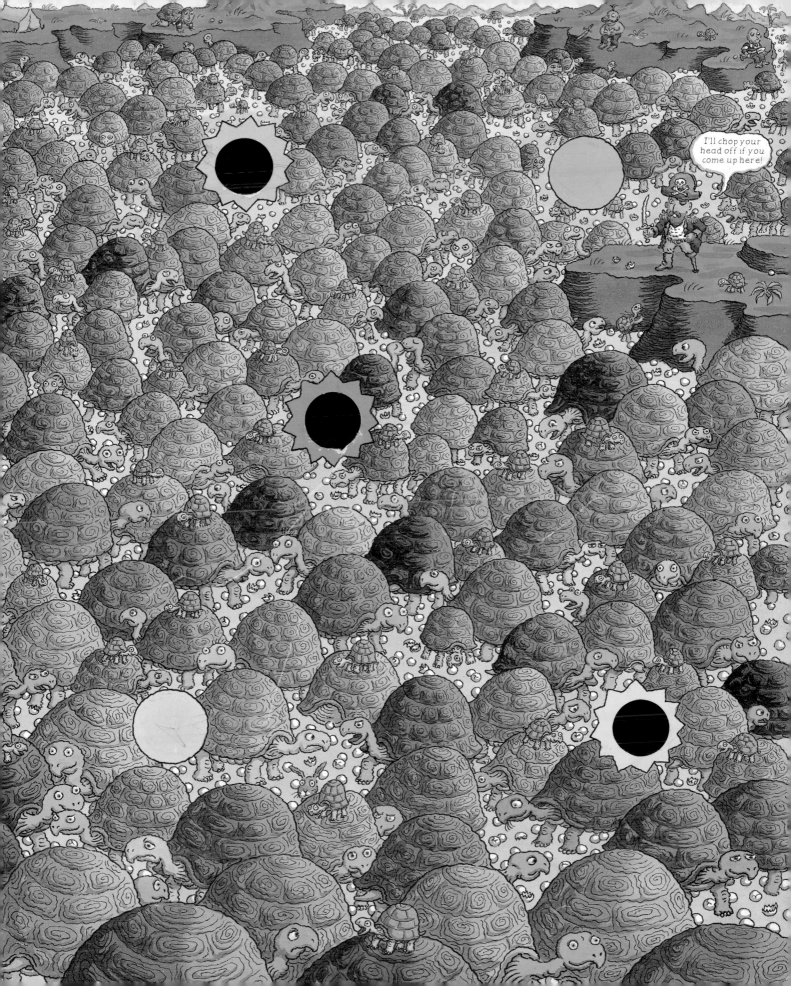

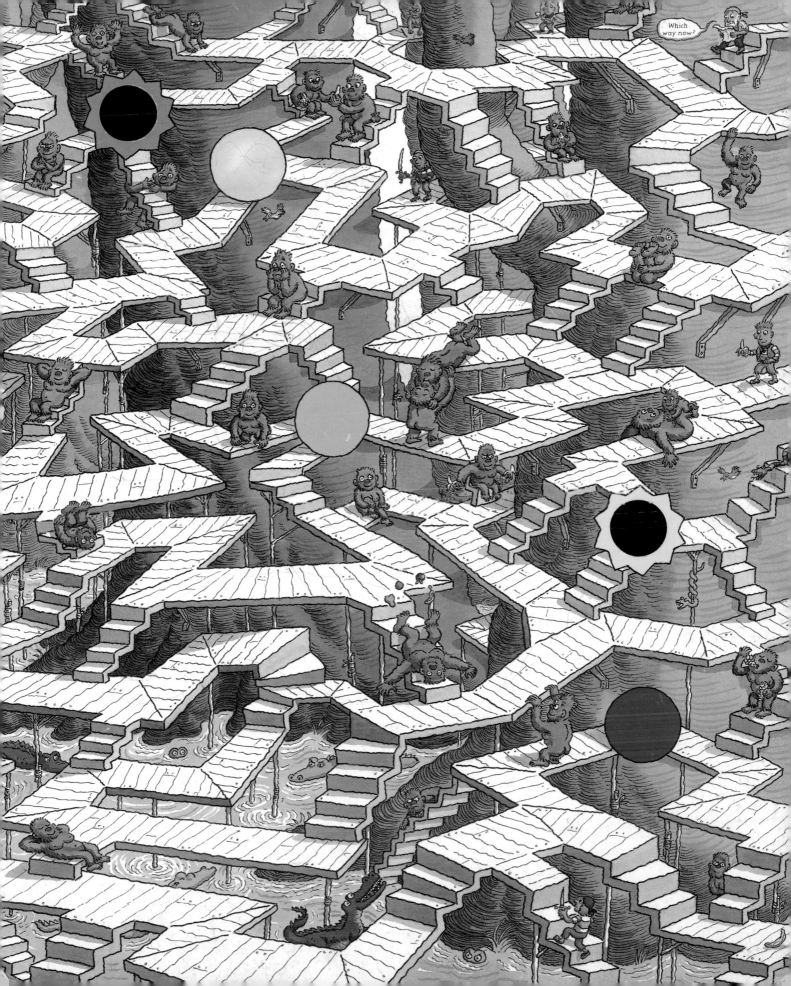

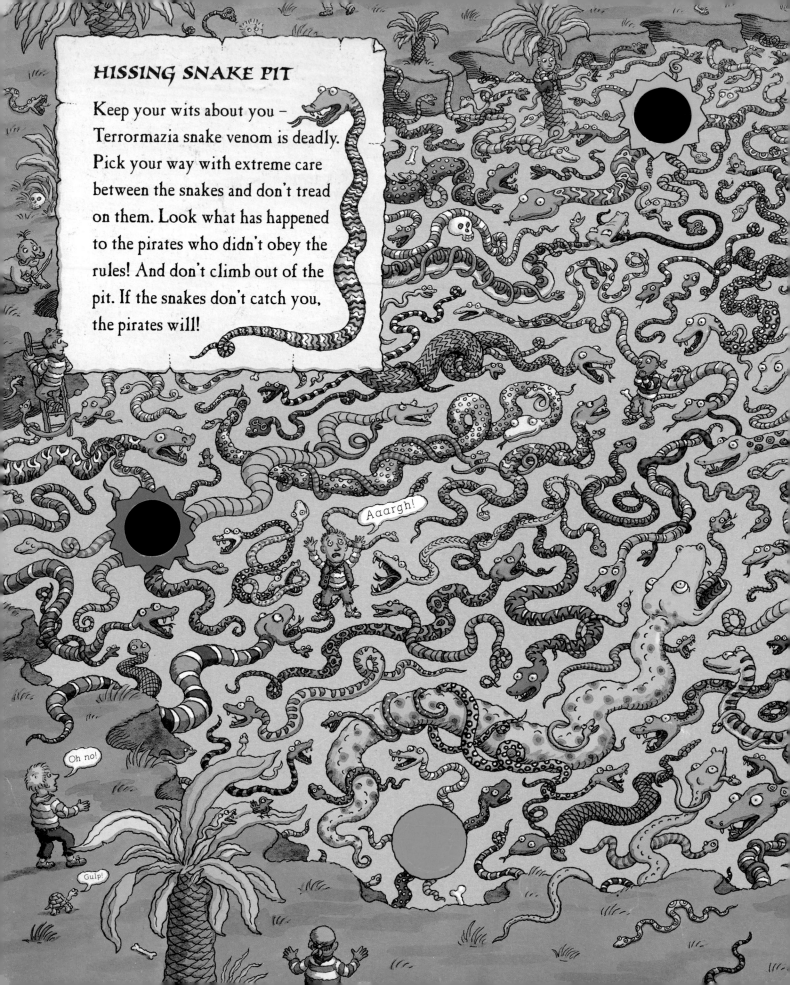

HISSING SNAKE PIT

Keep your wits about you –
Terrormazia snake venom is deadly.
Pick your way with extreme care
between the snakes and don't tread
on them. Look what has happened
to the pirates who didn't obey the
rules! And don't climb out of the
pit. If the snakes don't catch you,
the pirates will!

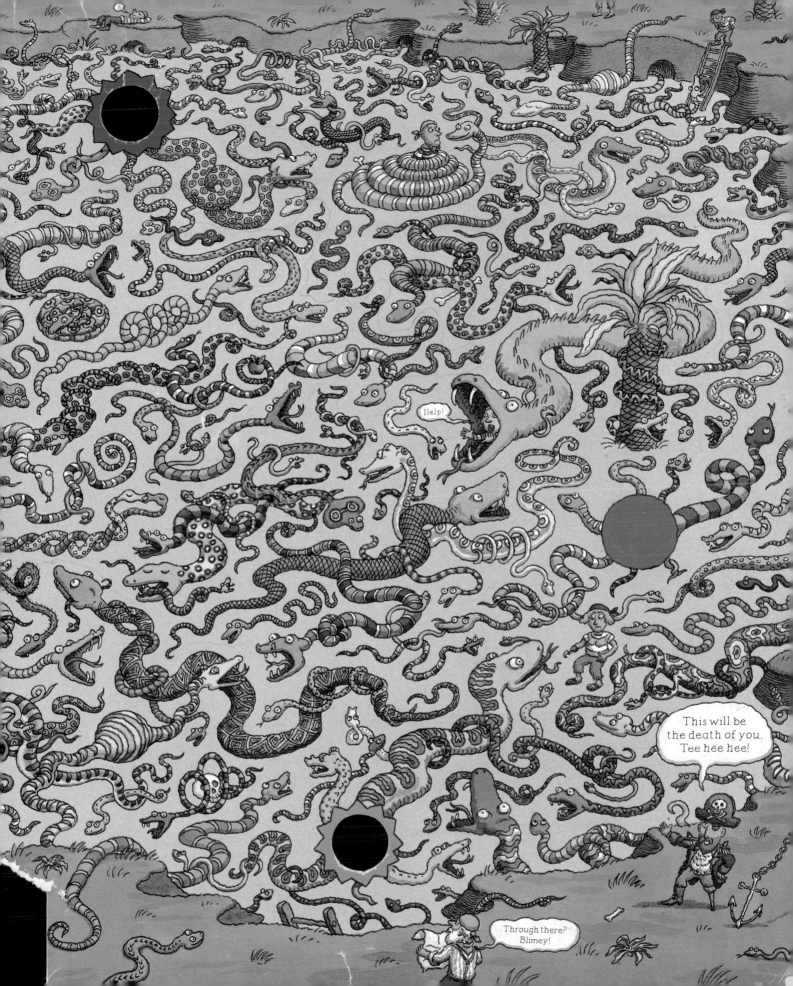

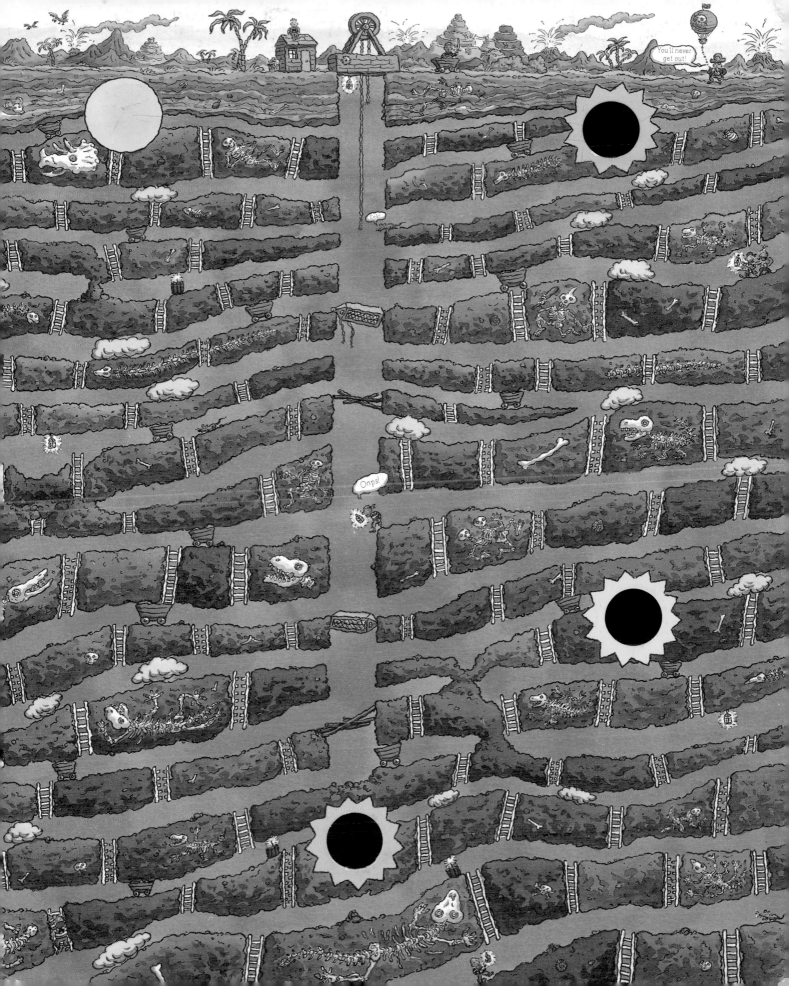

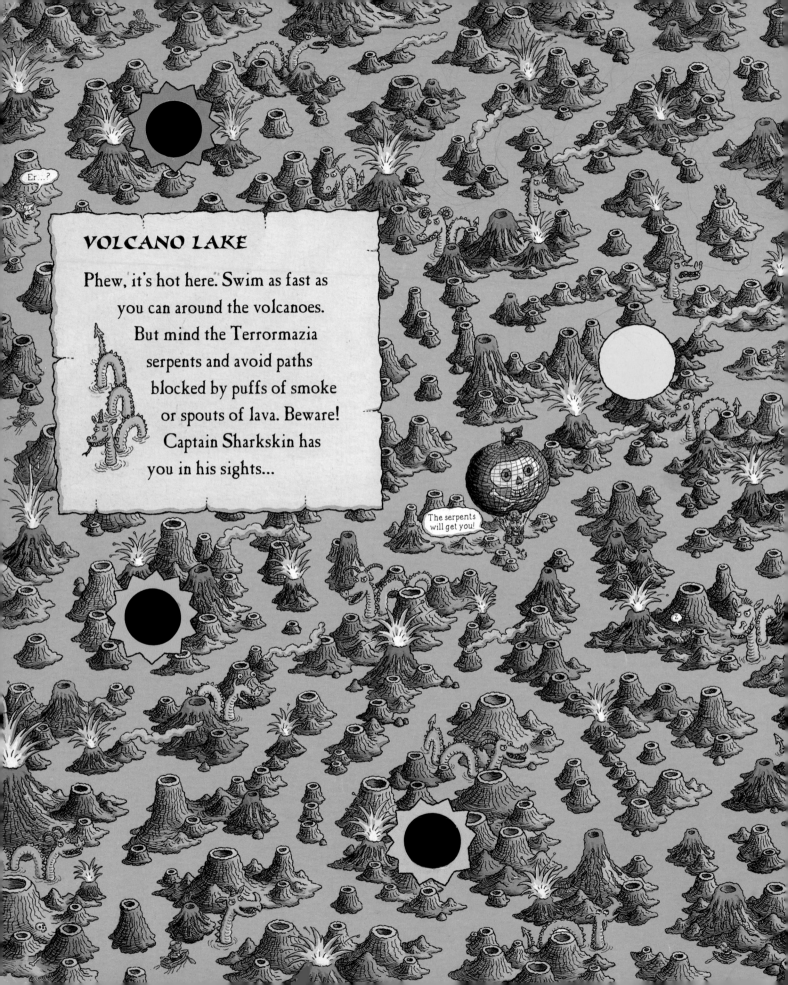

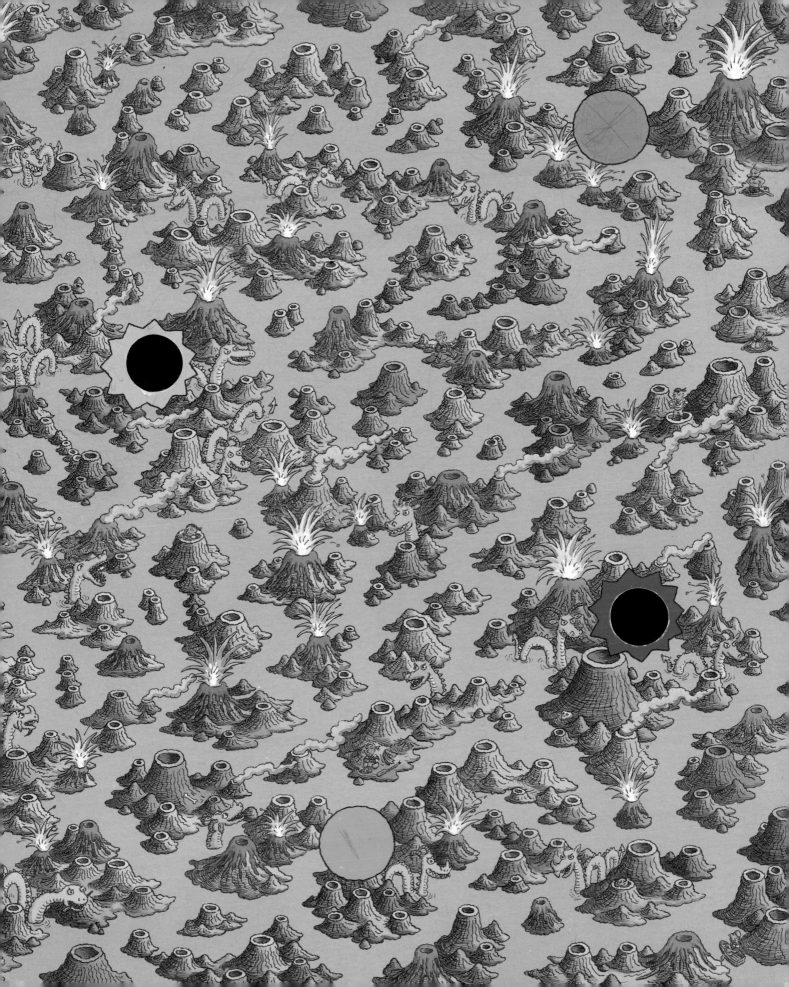

WEB OF WOE

Ugh! You've landed in the web of the giant Terrormazia spiders. Cling to the huge threads and get out as quickly as possible. Avoid broken threads and threads blocked by skeletons, trapped bodies, spiders or pirate bits and pieces. And don't cross the blood-stains or the spiders will pounce...

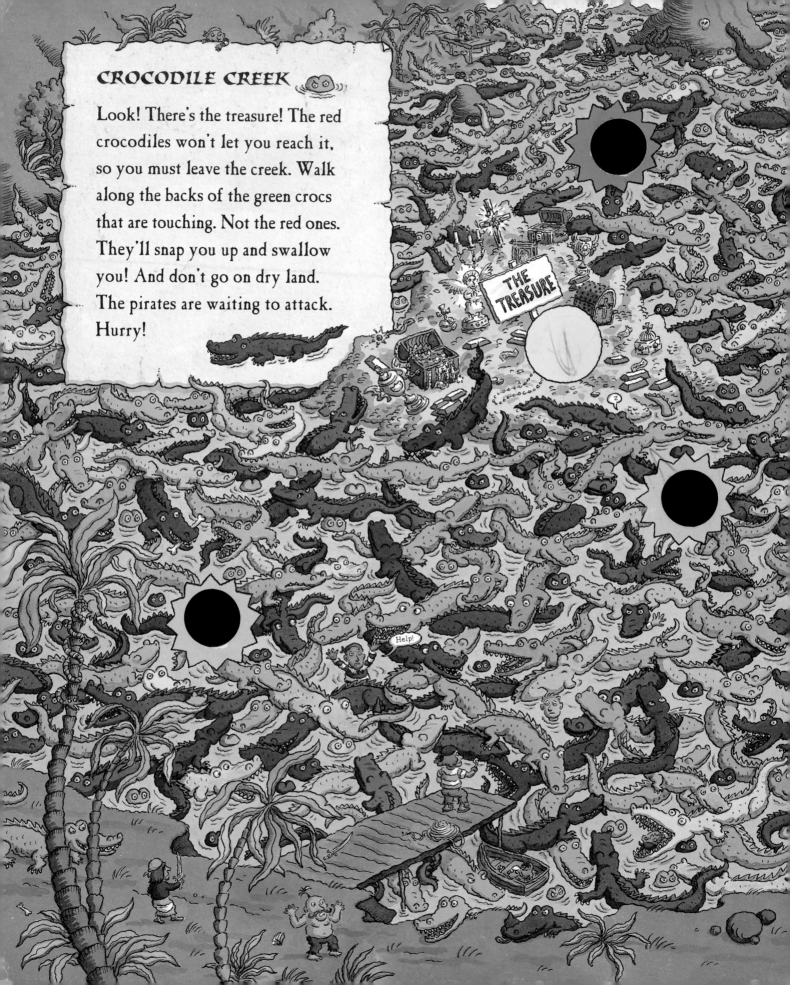

CROCODILE CREEK

Look! There's the treasure! The red
crocodiles won't let you reach it,
so you must leave the creek. Walk
along the backs of the green crocs
that are touching. Not the red ones.
They'll snap you up and swallow
you! And don't go on dry land.
The pirates are waiting to attack.
Hurry!

THE TREASURE

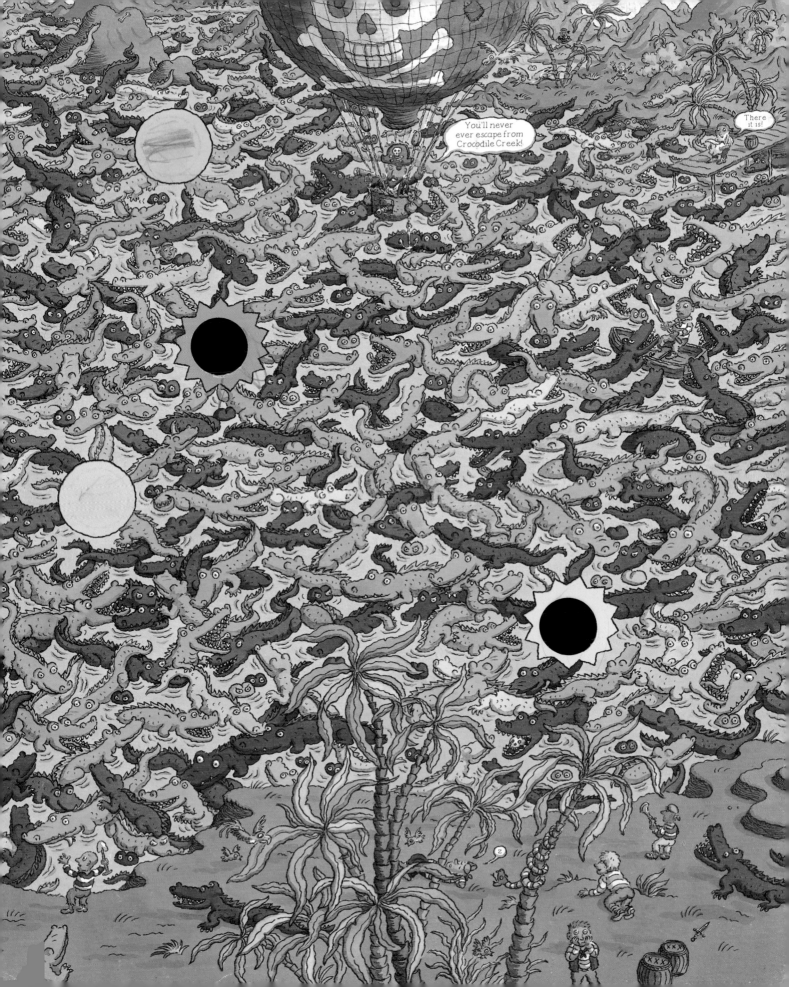

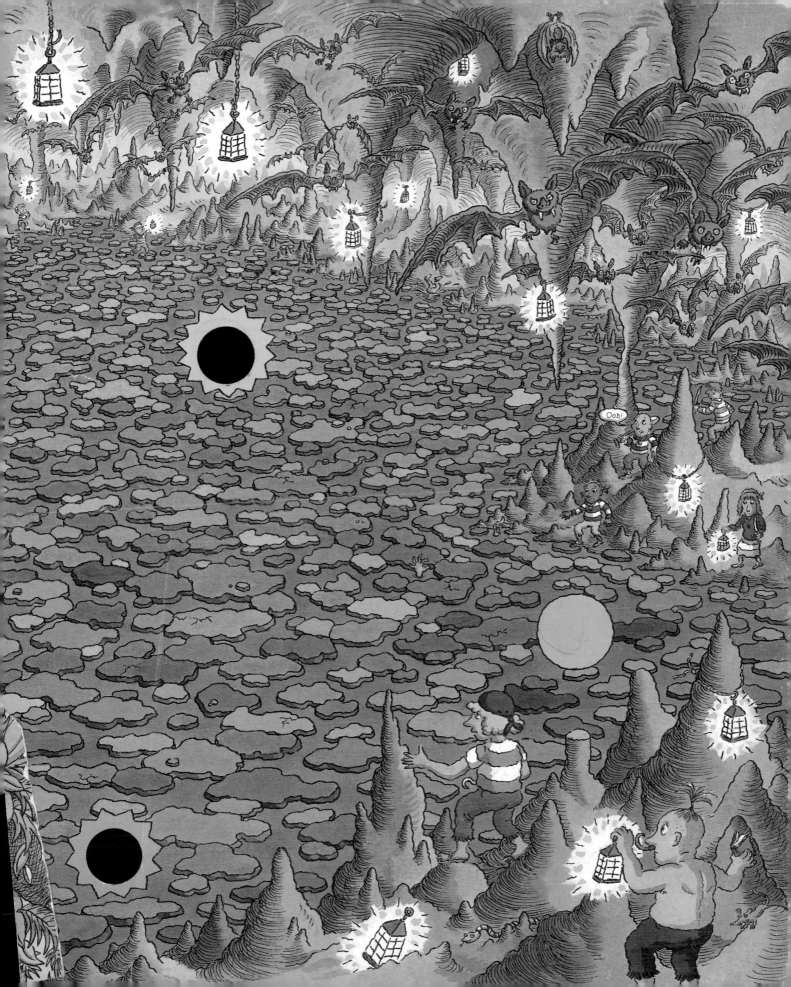

FATAL FOREST

You are up in the branches of the Fatal Forest. You can find a route by hopping from leaf to leaf. If you meet a pirate, hurry past! But tread only on the smooth leaves that touch. The spiky ones are poisonous. So are the tree trunks. One sting and you'll die.

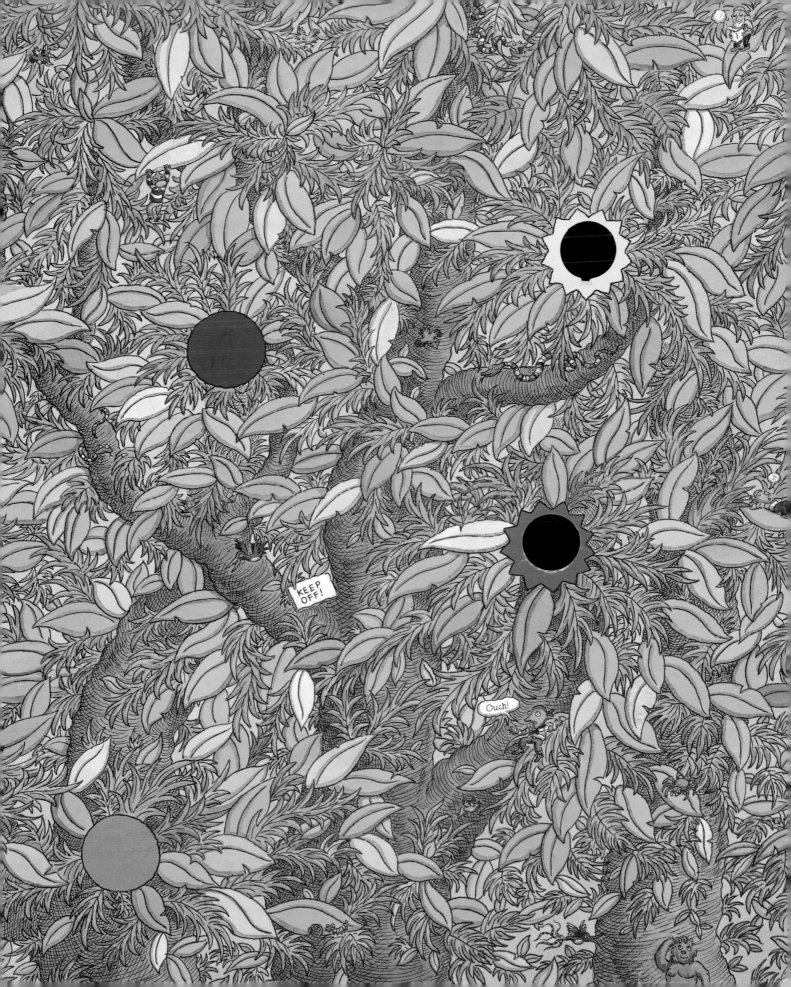

BAFFLING BONEYARD

You have arrived at the Baffling Boneyard. Pick your way carefully between these pirate remains but don't touch them. If you do, the ghosts of dead pirates may just rise up and get you. Oh, and the worms are looking hungry. Get out of here as quickly as you can!

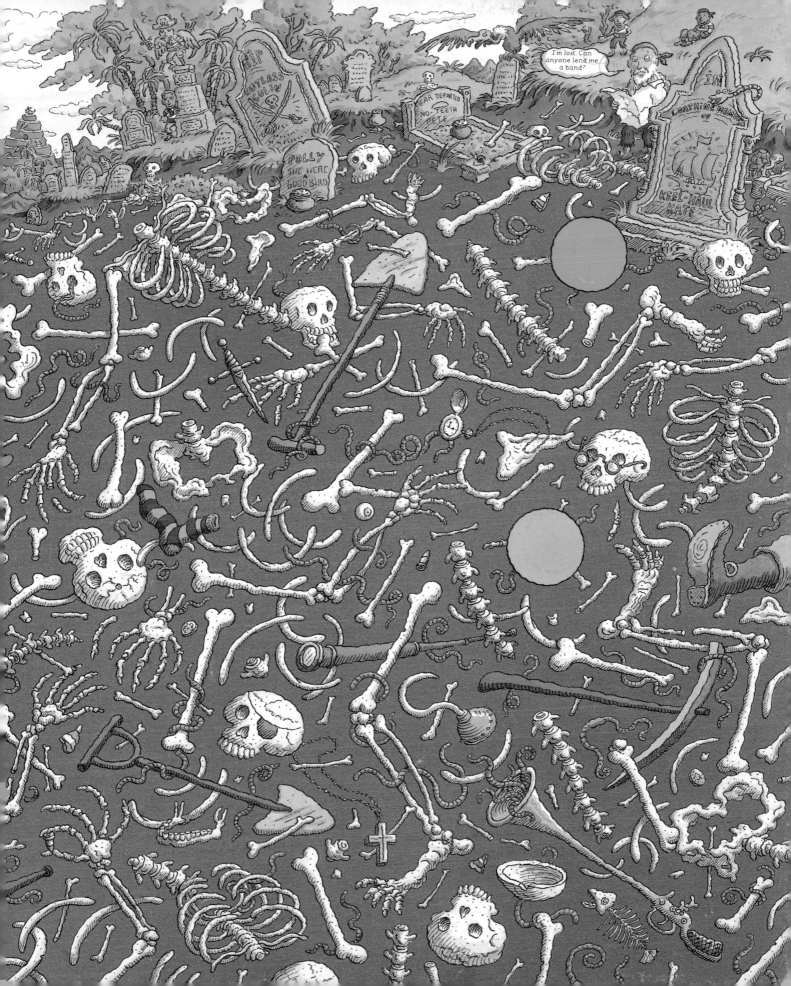

LOOK OUT FOR:

Mousemazia

written by
ANNA NILSEN

illustrated by
DOM MANSELL